A/RA-5 Vigilante
Mini in action

By Terry Love

Color By Don Gr & Tom Tullis

Illustrated By Joe Sewell

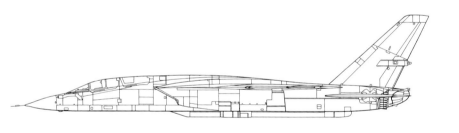

Mini Number 3

squadron/signal publications

This pair of RA-5C Vigilantes were assigned to RVAH-5, home based at NAS Key West Florida.

Acknowledgments

I want to acknowledge John E. Calhoun III, and Larry Mullaly - two Vigilante crew members par excellence! And to Carol Love, my wife, who put up with my enthusiasm about the Vigilante!

Al Adcock	John E. Calhoun III
Jim Goodall	Bob Lawson
Jim Mesko	Charles B. Mayer
Larry Mullaly	The Tailhook Society
Nicholas J. Waters III	

The Catapult Officer gives the go signal to this RA-5C of RVAH-5 as it prepares to launch from the bow catapult of USS AMERICA (CVA-66) on 15 October 1965. (USN via Jim Goodall)

ISBN 0-89747-329-0

If you have any photographs of aircraft, armor, soldiers or ships of any nation, particularly wartime snapshots, why not share them with us and help make Squadron/Signal's books all the more interesting and complete in the future. Any photograph sent to us will be copied and the original returned. The donor will be fully credited for any photos used. Please send them to

Если у вас есть фотографии самолётов, вооружения, солдат или кораблей любой страны, особенно, снимки времён войны, поделитесь с нами и помогите сделать новые книги издательства Эскадрон/Сигнал ещё интереснее. Мы переснимем ваши фотографии и вернём оригиналы. Имена приславших снимки будут сопровождать все опубликованные фотографии. Присылайте, пожалуйста, фотографии по адресу:

軍用機、装甲車両、兵士、軍艦などの写真を所持しておられる方はいらっしゃいませんか？どの国のものでも結構です。作戦中に撮影されたものが特に良いのです。Squadron/Signal社の出版する刊行物において、このような写真は内容を一層充実し、興味深くすることができます。当方にお送り頂いた写真は、複写の後お返しいたします。出版物中に写真を使用した場合は、必ず提供者のお名前を明記させて頂きます。お写真は下記にご送付ください。

Squadron/Signal Publications, Inc.
1115 Crowley Drive
Carrollton, TX 75011-5010 USA

3

Introduction

The Vigilante was intended as a high performance attack aircraft with all-weather capability. The A-5 had a high-wing layout and the low aspect ratio, swept-back wing was a typical North American Aviation design feature. The Vigilante probably introduced more new and advanced designed features than any other aircraft in history. Additionally, it was so capable (in a role quite different from that for which it was designed) that its withdrawal from active service left a gap the U. S. Navy could not fill.

During January of 1954, using the acronym NAGPAW (North American General Purpose Attack Weapon), North American Aviation conceived the idea for a basic design incorporating such advanced features as a linear bomb bay, with a rearward-ejection release system that was capable of functioning in the LABS (Low Altitude Bombing System) or toss bombing role. It also featured a nose-mounted radar to locate targets, and a proposed twin-jet engine layout. The U. S. Navy's Bureau of Aeronautics (BuAir) found the North American NA-233 design to be complimentary to its arguments for a super-carrier Navy nuclear deterrent force.

Submitted to the U.S. Navy at the end of 1954, the NA-233 was given a favorable reception. But two significant amendments to the proposed performance were requested by the Navy. First it was considered essential that NAGPAW should have supersonic performance to escape a nuclear blast (Mach 2 if possible). Secondly, it was required to have a capability for a full load take-off with zero wind over the deck with the use of catapults.

Since this zero-wind over the deck rarely, if ever, occurs, because the carrier is always underway when launching aircraft, this latter requirement seemed hard to justify. Luckily, this requirement was eventually relaxed. The Mach 2 performance was considered to be the primary objective.

This change occurred during January of 1955, and at this point NAGPAW was quickly revised to meet the new Navy specifications. The revised proposal was submitted to the Bureau of Aeronautics (BuAir) by North American in April of 1955. A letter of intent was received by North American on 29 June 1956 covering engineering, production, tooling and long lead time equipment for two YA3J-1 prototype/service test aircraft. BuAir wanted a nuclear-armed aircraft to replace or compliment the North American AJ Savage, the Lockheed P-2 Neptune, and the Douglas A-3 Skywarrior. In the design of the Vigilante, particular attention was paid to achieving a minimal cross section for super-sonic speed. The outcome of this was a small radar cross section (RCS), although stealth techniques had not been identified by the design team. The Vigilante, being a very large aircraft and very heavy aircraft, would have been a prime candidate for variable geometry swing-wings, but at the time this technology was unavailable to the design team,. The Grumman XF10F had only recently persuaded the Navy that this idea was too advanced a concept for industry at the time.

The Vigilante full-scale mock-up was quite similar to the actual aircraft with the exception of the air intakes, the rear cockpit canopy and twin vertical tail surfaces. (Tailhook)

4

The rollout of the YA3J-1 Vigilante (BuNo 145157) prototype took place on 16 May 1958 at the North American Aviation facilities in Columbus, Ohio. (Tailhook)

The small high loaded wing was made possible by the use of powerful flaps, the elimination of the ailerons (roll control being effected by the differential tail planes). The one-piece powered vertical tail (or all moving fin), fully variable engine inlets with profile as well as area adjustments to suit flight Mach numbers, internal weapons storage, a slim fuselage configured for Mach 2, were just some of the advanced features designed into the Vigilante. The aircraft also utilized one-piece wing skins machined from aluminum-lithium alloy, a fully retractable refueling probe in the forward fuselage, it used pure Nitrogen instead of hydraulic fluid in some of the hottest parts of the airframe, some major structures and frames were built out of Titanium, and a one-piece, bird-proof Mach 2 capable windshield made of stretched acrylics. The aircraft also featured computerized fly-by-wire flight controls and gold-plate in the engine bays to reflect heat. The engine inlets were sharp tipped and swept back for peak supersonic efficiency, with front and rear ramps to control the internal profile and throat area.

In order to keep the aircraft within the carrier hanger height limit, the aircraft was originally configured with twin vertical tail surfaces that were canted outward (similar to the McDonnell-Douglas F/A-18). This configuration was a bit hard for the U.S. Navy of 1955 to accept, although with the fuselage width, there would have been no problem. Reluctantly, the North American team was persuaded to use a single vertical center-line fin, and make the top of the fin foldable to meet the hanger bay requirement.

Among the many "firsts" on the Vigilante was the first use of an airborne digital computer for bomb and navigation computations. Also the first Bomb-Nav System with an inertial auto-navigation coupled to radar and television-sights for check point verification. The Vigilante had the first heads-up display (HUD), the first fully integrated auto pilot/air data system for Bomb/Nav weapons release, the first monopulse radar with terrain avoidance features, the first variable inlet using horizontal ramp geometry, and the first production fly-by-wire control systems.

The word Vigilante means "one who is watchful and ever alert to danger". The Vigilante was the last strategic bomber built for the Navy. The aircraft was truly a pioneer, but it was designed for the wrong war. Much like the U.S. Air Force's Convair B-58 Hustler, it fell victim to a changing requirement, designed to also fly at high altitude and supersonic speeds both became highly vulnerable to the vastly improved anti-aircraft missiles then entering service.

The Vigilante was big, beautiful and powerful. It was an impressive airplane to behold. A great deal of Titanium was used in the aircraft's construction, some 2,400 pounds of it, mostly in the tubular engine-bay housings. All Vigilantes were built at North American Aviation's Columbus, Ohio plant.

Every system on the Vigilante could be operated simultaneously regardless of speed. There was no loss of quality as the speed increased. Because the aircraft was originally configured as a bomber, the Vigilante carried plenty of fuel to enable it to fly in continuous afterburner on every mission, and

The first flight of the YA3J-1 occurred on 31 August 1958 with company chief test pilot Dick Wenzel at the controls. The chase plane was a NAA FJ-4 Fury fighter. (Tailhook)

not be worried about fuel while waiting to land back aboard the carrier. Other aircraft were forced to fly burdened by missiles, gun-pods and fuel drop tanks slung underneath them. The weight and drag of these stores drastically shortened their range. The Vigilante had no problems in this area.

The YA3J-1, Vigilante number one (BuNo 145157), flew for the first time on 31 August 1958 with Dick Wenzel, North American Aviation's test pilot, at the controls. It was powered by two YJ79-GE-2 turbojet engines. The roll out took place on 16 May 1958 at which time the aircraft was officially named Vigilante.

The crew of the Vigilante flew in tandem in twin cockpits equipped with North American HS-1 rocket ejection seats. One unique feature of the aircraft was the linear bomb bay, basically a tunnel running lengthwise in the rear fuselage between the engines. The stores in the bomb bay being ejected rearward. The bay was equipped with rails, a catapult, and stored a free-fall nuclear weapon at the forward end. The weapons launching system triggered a series of latches that released the disposable tail cone before the weapon was released. The bomb was attached to two large fuel tanks (on a mission the fuel was used from these tanks first) and the empty tanks were ejected with the bomb and acted as aerodynamic stabilizers for the free-fall to the target. The bay was flexible in that it could carry other systems like reconnaissance collections,

auxiliary fuel tanks, and other "special" equipment packages. In service; however, the rearward bomb ejection system never did work very well, and bombs released had a tendency to trail behind the aircraft for a long distance before actually falling free, making bombing accuracy impossible.

Rarely has a military aircraft found itself performing in a role for which it was never intended. The North American A-5 Vigilante was one such aircraft. In order to operate from carriers, the Vigilante had to incorporate a great many complex systems. These met the high performance requirements, but the aircraft could not carry a large enough non-nuclear conventional payload to warrant a large scale production. The Navy soon realized that its strategic role would be better served with submarine launched ballistic missiles.

The Navy's decision to abandon airborne nuclear strike cast considerable doubt on the future of the Vigilante program for some time. Despite a relatively trouble-free development, the Vigilante was not ordered into production until 1959. These were intended to be conventional strike aircraft. It is ironic that the Vigilante survived because of its low-level capabilities, which had earlier been compromised by the Navy's demand for Mach 2 speed. The Vigilante's first carrier landing was made aboard the USS SARATOGA on 22 July 1960, bringing the Navy into the Mach 2 world.

Development

A3J-1/A-5A

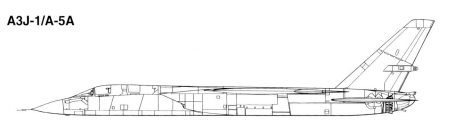

A3J-2/A-5B

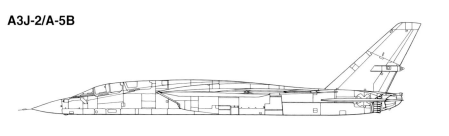

RA-5C (Early)

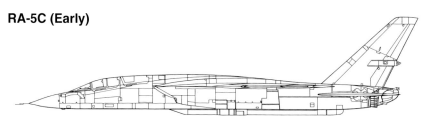

RA-5C (Late)

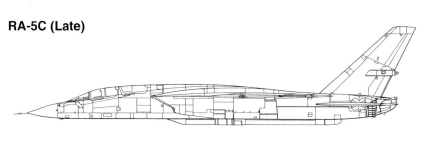

A3J-1/A-5A Vigilante

The first production A3J-1 Vigilantes joined the test program during 1960. The production A3J-1 differed from the YA3J-1s in their power plants. Initial aircraft in the production run had the same engines as the YA3J-1, the J79-GE-2, but these were quickly supplanted at an early stage in the production run by the J79-GE-4 and finally the definitive J79-GE-8 engines. These were the identical engines used by the McDonnell-Douglas F-4B, F-4J, F-4N and F-4S series of jet fighters, making the parts supply problem aboard ship much easier to handle.

Early production A3J-1s completed initial carrier trials aboard the USS SARATOGA during July of 1960. These car-quals went very smoothly, since it was found that the Vigilante was very much at home in carrier operations at sea.

North American and several major factions in the Navy considered the Vigilante an extraordinary aircraft, and one very much worth promoting. To highlight the Navy's claims during the first stages of what was soon to become a bitter fight with Congress to keep the Vigilante program alive, early production examples of the aircraft were utilized to set several world speed and altitude records. In the former category, noted aviatrix and then president of the Federation Aeronautique Internationale (FAI), Jacqueline Cochran, became the first woman to fly Mach 2, as an occupant of the Bombardier/Navigator's (BNs) compartment on 6 June 1960. She participated in a speed run over southern Ohio that reached Mach 2.02 at 47,000 feet.

This record was followed by a new world altitude record for the class when on 13 December 1960, a Vigilante carried a 1,000 kg (2,402.62 pound) payload on a zoom profile flight that peaked at 91,451 feet. The crew for this flight was Navy Commander Leroy Heath and Lieutenant Larry Monroe, both of the Naval Air Test Center. Commander Heath was awarded the Distinguished Flying Cross while Lieutenant Monroe received the Air Medal.

These four operational A3J-1s were assigned to VAH-3, and were formally handed over at NAS Sanford on 16 June 1961. The first fully operational unit to receive the Vigilante was VAH-7 Peacemakers, which took delivery of their first aircraft on 25 January 1962. The unit subsequently underwent carrier qualifications aboard the USS FRANKLIN D. ROOSEVELT (CVA-42) before participating in the shakedown cruise

The first production A3J-1 Vigilante reveals its very sleek lines and broad flat fuselage. The aircraft was built for speed and it easily went Mach 1 plus. (Tailhook)

This A3J-1 (BuNo 146696) was used to conduct live ejection seat tests during 1959. This aircraft was the fifth Vigilante off the production line and it was later converted to the RA-5C configuration. (Tailhook)

of the first nuclear-powered aircraft carrier, USS ENTERPRISE (CVAN-65) in February of 1962. "Heavy Seven" subsequently became the first Vigilante squadron to deploy operationally when it embarked for a brief Mediterranean cruise aboard the ENTERPRISE during August of 1962. The cruise was cut short in October due to the Cuban Missile Crisis, when the ENTERPRISE with her load of Vigilantes quickly steamed back to the Eastern Atlantic to support operations off Cuba.

The second deployable squadron to receive the Vigilante was VAH-1 Smokin' Tigers. The squadron began its transition program in September of 1962 under the guidance of VAH-3 although it was not until 22 January 1963 that the unit took delivery of its first A-5A (as the A3J-1 became known after the DOD reorganization of the designations). They were then attached to USS INDEPENDENCE (CVA-62), making just one Mediterranean deployment with this Vigilante variant.

Catapult launch in the A-5A was always an adventure, particularly when fully loaded

This A3J-1 (BuNo 147855) carried special Red markings while assigned to Naval Air Special Weapons Facility at Kirkland Air Force Base, New Mexico during August of 1961. The Vigilante crashed during these tests. (USN via Charles B. Mayer)

9

A3J-1/A-5A Weapons Delivery System

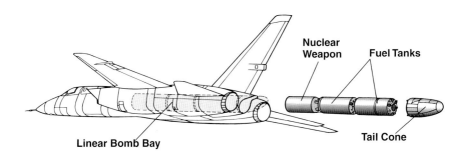

Nuclear Weapon
Fuel Tanks
Linear Bomb Bay
Tail Cone

(Above) This A3J-1 (BuNo 147863) of Heavy Attack Squadron Three (VAH-3), was the twenty-fifth Vigilante built and was delivered from the factory in the standard Navy color scheme of Gloss Gull Gray over Gloss White. The aircraft was lost on 27 September 1964. (Tailhook)

(Below) During 1962, VAH-7 carried these squadron markings while assigned to USS ENTERPRISE (CVAN-65) BuNo 149283 was later converted to the RA-5C configuration and was shot down over North Vietnam on 18 May 1968. (Tailhook)

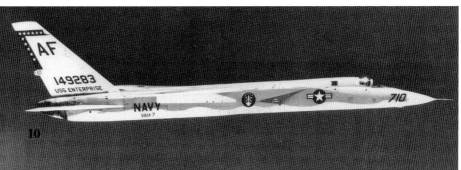

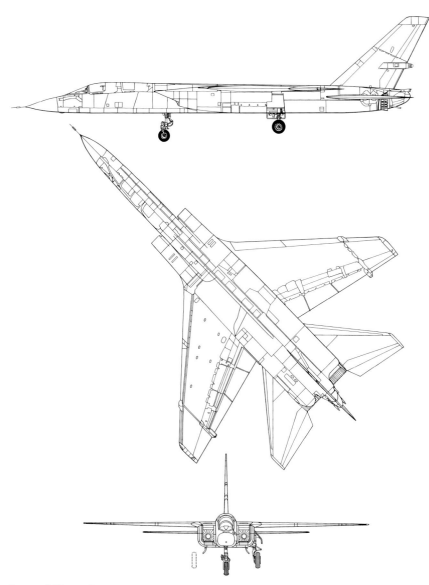

Specification

North Amrican A-5A Vigilante

Wingspan..............53.2 feet (16.21 m**)**
Length..................76.55 feet (23.33 m**)**
Height....................19.37 feet (5.90 m)
Empty Weight.......32,714 pounds (14,839 kg)
Maximum Weight..56,293 pounds (25,534.5 kg)
Powerplant............Two 16,500 lbst J79-GE-8 turbojet engines.
Armament..............One Nuclear Weapon

Speed...................1,320 mph (2,124 kph)
Service Ceiling....52,100 feet (15,880 m)
Range..................1,807 miles (2,908 km)
Crew.................. ..Two

This A3J-1 BuNo 148930 of VAH-3 folds its outer wing panels as it prepares to be respotted on the flight deck during flight operations as sea in 1962. In addition to the folding outer wing panels, the vertical stabilizer folded over on its side to allow the aircraft to be stored in the hanger bay. (Jim Mesko)

This A3J-1/A-5A (BuNo 147863) of VAH-3 was being towed on the deck by a Yellow tug during 1962. The aircraft was manned by the plane captain who "rode the brakes" to prevent the aircraft from rolling out of control. The aircraft boarding ladder was still in place on the port side of the fuselage. (Jim Mesko)

with fuel cells in the linear bomb bay. The tremendous acceleration of the launch could jar the fuel cells from their position and, if they broke free cleanly, there would be a spectacular fire on the flight deck. If; however, some of the one ton fuel cells tore the plumbing out of adjacent cells and started an onboard fire, then the aircraft was usually lost.

In practice, the Vigilante settled into carrier-borne operations quite well despite being mainly restricted to the larger vessels. In fact, the only serious shortcoming involved the unique linear bomb bay. In simple terms it consisted of a tube running along the fuselage, weapons loading being effected via an opening at the extreme tail between the jet exhausts. Weapons ejection was also effected via this opening with a solid fuel cartridge being used to propel the device clear of the aircraft once the jettisonable tail-cone fairing had been ejected. Since the weapons bay was considerably longer than the nuclear weapons which the Vigilante was

originally intended to carry it was decided to utilize some of this space for additional fuel. This fuel was contained in two jettisonable tanks located aft of the weapon and linked to it. They were also ejected and fulfilled the additional function of stabilizing the device during its fall. Although a viable system in theory, the system did not work well in reality and this eventually led to a decision in early 1962, to modify the Vigilante for the specialized tactical reconnaissance role.

After this decision was made, the A-5As were quickly relegated training roles and removed from the active inventory as heavy attack aircraft. At a later date, all surviving airframes were returned to the North American plant at Columbus for conversion to RA-5C standards.

Production of the A3J-1/A-5A was completed by early 1963, when the production line began tooling up for the A-5B, which was easily switched to the RA-5C, the ultimate Vigilante variant.

(Above) The A3J was very successful during carrier qualifications, which began on 20 July 1960 aboard the USS SARATOGA (CVA-60). With its large trailing edge flaps in the full down position, this A3J-1 leaves the angle deck and begins its climb out. . (Naval Aviation Museum)

(Below) BuNo 147863 was next In line for launch from the port bow catapult during at sea operations in 1962. Just in front of the aircraft (MODEX) number, 257, on the wing flap are the open slots for the engine bleed air that blows high pressure air over the flaps, giving the aircraft additional lift. (Jim Mesko)

13

A-5B Vigilante

During 1961, North American began studying means of extending the Vigilante's range and load-carrying capabilities. Two growth versions of the A-5A were proposed, the first of these, the A-5B, was, like its predecessor, intended primarily for the attack role, and the second, the RA-5C was essentially a reconnaissance aircraft (retaining attack capabilities).

Formally, the A3J-2/A-5B was an interim long range version which evolved from the A-5A. It had no change in its mission, but introduced substantial airframe modifications aimed at increasing range and payload. The most obvious change between the A-5A and A-5B was the raising of the fuselage spine which gave the Vigilante a pronounced humped-back appearance. This raised section made room for an enormous increase in the internal fuel capacity of the Vigilante. Other modifications included increasing both the span and the chord of the trailing edge flaps to give a much larger square-foot area (and increased lift). Another modification was changes to the inboard wing structure to allow the aircraft to carry four underwing weapons/fuel pylons which were capable of carrying 2,000 pounds each. Typical stores included 400 U.S. gallon fuel tanks, nuclear or conventional bombs, Bullpup missiles or other stores. Also added were a pair of high intensity strobe lights which were mounded under the wings for night illumination.

Less obvious, but no less significant, were changes to the aircraft's braking capacity (due to the increased weight) and in the size and shape of the inlet ducts, the latter changes being specifically intended to enhance performance at high speed and high altitude.

Coupled with the increased power of the J79-GE-8 engines and some other engine improvements, this allowed the gross weight of the Vigilante to be increased by some 10,000 pounds to about 80,000 pounds. A modification of the boundary layer control system to blow high-pressure engine bleed air over the top surfaces of the wing from the front instead of the rear portion as on the A-5A, allowed all of the additional weight on the A-5B to be minimized.

The single seat A-5B/A3J-2 prototype (BuNo 146694) was the third A-5A airframe. The aircraft was used for the conversion to the A-5B configuration which had numerous improvements over the A-5A designed to improve the aircraft's performance and particularly its range. (Tailhook)

The second A3J-2 prototype (BuNo 146699) was rolled out on 20 June 1962. the chief difference between the A3J-1 and A3J-2, the fuel hump back, is clearly evident. This aircraft was modified from the eighth A-5A airframe. (Tailhook)

The first A-5B (BuNo 149300) flew on 29 April 1962. Eighteen A-5Bs were ordered, but by that time the Navy's reconnaissance requirement resulted in a reduction of the Vigilantes production effort. The first six A3J-2s were too far along in the production process to be quickly reconfigured to the reconnaissance configuration. Of these, only two (BuNo 149300 and 149301) were delivered to the Navy as A-5Bs The other four (BuNos 149302, 149303, 149304 and 149305) were delivered as YA-5Cs. These four were utilized by VAH-3 in an interim role as RA-5C trainers during late 1963. The remaining twelve A-5Bs, and all other A-5Bs, were later converted to RA-5C standards.

Since the jet engines were at the rear of the aircraft, the bleed air from them was routed up to the leading edge of the wings for the hot high-pressure air system via a pipe under the wing root. A noticeable fairing was added for this pipe, however, the route of the piping was later modified for the production RA-5C.

Considerable difficulties were encountered in clearing the linear bomb bay for operational use and before these could be satisfactorily overcome. A major shift in Navy policy deleted the strategic bombing role.

Fuselage Development

A3J-1/A-5A

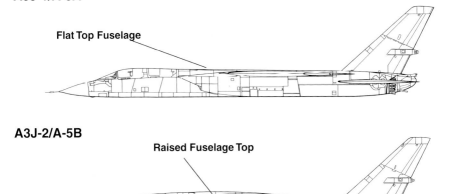

Flat Top Fuselage

A3J-2/A-5B

Raised Fuselage Top

Blown Flap Duct Fairing

This A3J-2/A-5B displays the weapons it was cleared to carry on the four underwing fuel/weapons pylons, leaving the linear bomb bay clear for additional fuel and nuclear weapons options. (Tailhook)

Consequently plans to produce the improved Vigilante attack-bomber were abandoned after it had reached the flight-test phase. It had been decided to standardize on the RA-5C, for which a number of A-5Bs subse-

quently served as development aircraft. There were no A-5Bs were delivered to active U.S. Navy squadrons for fleet service.

This A3J-2/A-5B on a test flight reveals the underwing root fairing that housed the plumbing for the engine air bleed system for the wing leading edge slats. None of the A3J-2/A-5Bs ever had the ventral camera canoe fitted. (Tailhook)

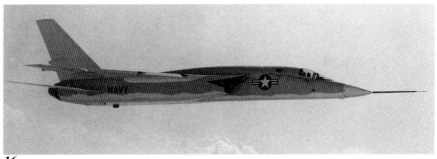

RA-5C Vigilante

The RA-5C flew for the first time on 30 June 1962. It embodied the same modifications that had been incorporated into the A-5B with a few minor changes. The chief difference was the addition of a reconnaissance pod in the former weapons bay and a long external underfuselage pod called the "canoe". The canoe had no adverse effect on the speed or performance of the Vigilante, and contained an extremely sophisticated optical/electronic reconnaissance system. A SLAR (Side Looking Airborne Radar) unit was installed and the aircraft's photographic equipment included vertical, oblique, split-image cameras, and horizon-to-horizon panoramic scanning cameras. The non-photographic equipment, in addition to the SLAR, included sensors in the infrared end radio region frequencies for gathering electro-magnetic intelligence (Passive Electronic Counter-measures [PECM]), and a television camera capable of functioning in very low light levels. The television was mounted under the nose just behind the radome. The associated electronic equipment was packaged in the linear weapons bay, and two high-intensity supersonic strobe-type flasher pods were mounted on the underwing pylons to illuminate the ground under the aircraft. Additionally, the RA-5C retained its capability for carrying underwing ordnance, although it was rarely, if ever, used.

The first RA-5C was delivered on 27 June 1963 and the aircraft entered service during 1964 when RVAH-5 took its aircraft aboard USS RANGER (CVA-65). The aircraft and squadron answered a U. S. Navy need for a capable, manned, long-range reconnaissance system to augment short range tactical systems, such as the RF-8G Crusader. This is why the RA-5C was developed.

All of the reconnaissance systems on the Vigilante worked together and recorded a flood of intelligence data. The RA-5C formed the airborne reconnaissance unit of the Integrated Operational Intelligence System (IOIS). All of this information was

The YA-5C (BuNo 149305) in a hangar at NAS South Weymouth, Massachusetts during September of 1963. The aircraft was "displayed" carrying VAH-3 markings. At the time the hot bleed air fairings were still carried on the wing root undersurface. This aircraft was later lost during the flight deck fire aboard the USS FORRESTALL (CVA-59) on 29 July 1967. (Tailhook)

Fuselage Development

A-5B

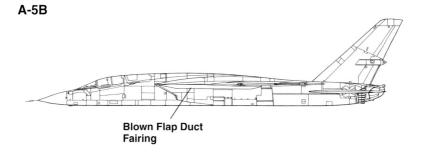

Blown Flap Duct
Fairing

RA-5C

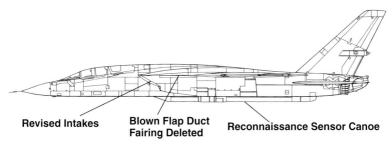

Revised Intakes

Blown Flap Duct
Fairing Deleted

Reconnaissance Sensor Canoe

instantly recorded on magnetic tape, which, together with the exposed photographic film was being brought back to the carrier for processing, read-out and analysis. This was the function of the Integrated Operational Intelligence Center (IOIC) aboard each carrier. Housed within the IOIC was an electronic intelligence data handling center, a one-hour photo processing center whose equipment (Kodak EH-38 high speed processors) was highly classified at the time (now this same type of equipment is readily available at most shopping malls for one-hour processing). After processing the film

One of two airframes converted to serve as the RA-5C prototypes. This aircraft was configured with a flight test nose probe, four underwing pylons and ventral reconnaissance system "canoe" on 10 October 1962. The outboard wing pylons are armed with Martin Marietta AGM-42 Bullpup missiles and the inboard pylons are carrying Mk 43 thermo nuclear "shapes" (training devices) on the inboard pylons. (Tailhook)

This RA-5C was used to conduct weapons pylons test configurations on 10 October 1962. The Vigilante was configured with twelve Mk 82 low drag bombs on Multiple Ejector Racks (MERs) on the outboard pylons, and two Mk 83 bombs on the inboard pylons. (Tailhook)

it was read out by enlisted specialists known as Photographic Intelligencemen (PTs). These men were specialists at interpretation of the the images on the Vigilantes reconnaissance film. Other specialists analyzed the electronic data for information on enemy radar and radio sites.

This reconnaissance system worked so well that all surviving A-5A and A-5B aircraft were returned to North American Aviation's Columbus, Ohio facilities to be modified to RA-5C standards. The demonstrated ability of the RA-5C to meet a long standing need for long range fleet reconnaissance now provided the justification to keep the Vigilante in production. The first purpose built RA-5C was BuNo 150823.

During the 1960s, a total of forty-three standard RA-5Cs were built, these following closely on the heels of the eighteen original A-5B aircraft. When the last of these rolled off of the Columbus, Ohio assembly line, it appeared that the Vigilante production had come to an end. Accordingly, tooling and related hardware was placed in long-term storage. The Columbus facility then shifted its priorities to other projects including the re-manufacture of the forty-three remaining A-5A and A-5B aircraft to RA-5C standards. But, attrition caused by the continuing hostilities over Vietnam resulted in renewed Navy interest in the RA-5C.

In 1967, the aircraft had proven remarkably successful in its reconnaissance role.

Deck handlers hook up the catapult bridals in preparation for launching this RVAH-5 Vigilante from the from the port bow catapult of the USS AMERICA (CVA-66) on 15 October 1965. BuNo 150836 is equipped with supersonic night photography electronic flasher pods under the wings. (USN via Jim Goodall)

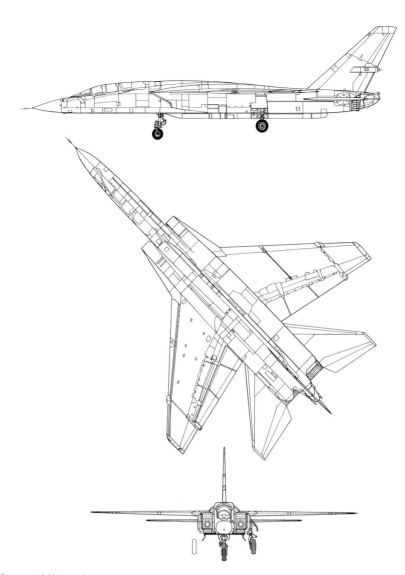

Specification

North Amrican RA-5C Vigilante

Wingspan..............53.2 feet (16.21 m**)**   **Speed**..................1.320 mph (2,124 kph)

Length...................76.55 feet (23.33 m**)**   **Service Ceiling**....52,100 feet (15,880 m)

Height....................19.37 feet (5.90 m)   **Range**..................2,050 miles 3,299 km)

Empty Weight.......37,489 pounds (17,005 kg)   **Crew**................. ..Two

Maximum Weight..79,588 pounds (36,101.1 kg)

Powerplant............Two 17,859 lbst J79-GE-10 turbojet engines.

Armament..............None

RA-5C Reconnaissance Systems

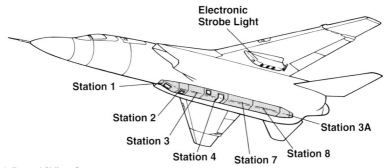

Electronic
Strobe Light

Station 1

Station 2

Station 3

Station 4

Station 7

Station 8

Station 3A

Station 1: Forward Oblique Camera
Station 2: Vertical Camera
Station 3: PECM Antenna
Station 4: Various Combinations of Panoramic Cameras, Vertical
Cameras, Oblique Cameras.
Station 7: Infrared Sensor
Station 8: Side Looking Radar (SLAR)
Station 3A: PECM Antenna

Since its information gathering capability could not be duplicated by any other aircraft, and no other readily available aircraft was capable for modification, the Navy, during 1968, in a very rare occurrence, reinstated the RA-5C production line. Although initial orders called for forty-six new production RA-5C, only thirty-six were actually built. The last totally new Vigilante was completed on 10 August 1970 (BuNo 156853).

The RA-5C was one of the most remarkable combat weapons ever introduced into the Navy's inventory. That claim can be made that, despite the fact that it was designed for the attack mission, for which it achieved little success and its career was short lived, that total production totaled only 156 aircraft including the prototypes and that unit costs were very high, approximately nine million dollars per aircraft. It was; however, the right aircraft, at the right time.

The thirty-six new-built RA-5Cs on the 1968 order, were all powered by J79-GE-10 engines, and had a leading edge extension (LEX) from the wing root to the forward air-intake lip.

A RA-5C of RVAH-3 performs a touch-and-go landing (the aircraft's tail hook was still in the raised position) during flight operations aboard the USS RANGER (CVA-61) in the Atlantic Ocean. (John Calhoun III)

The air intake of this RVAH-5 RA-5C reveals that this was an early production RA-5C powered by the J79-GE-8 engine. The curved leading edges of the intake are different on the inboard and outboard sides. This RA-5C was on the deck of the USS America (CVA-66) on 15 October 1965. (USN via Jim Goodall)

Air Intakes

RA-5C (Early)

RA-5C (Late)

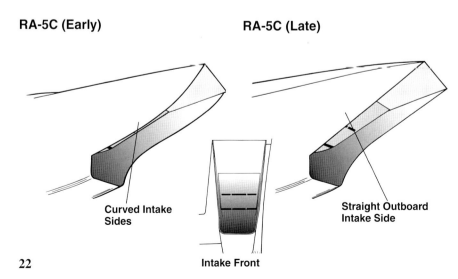

Curved Intake
Sides

Straight Outboard
Intake Side

Intake Front

This RA-5C (BuNo 149298) of RVAH-7 aboard USS KITTYHAWK (CVA-63) displays two of the major differences between the late production RA-5C and earlier variants of the Vigilante, the revised air intake and wing LEX (Leading Edge Extension). The inboard wing leading edge was extended all the way to the leading edge of the air intake. (Nicholas J. Waters III)

"Taking up the slack," catapult crews position a RA-5C of RVAH-5 on the port bow catapult of USS AMERICA (CVA-66) prior to launch during at sea operations in October of 1965. (USN via Jim Goodall)

Combat

The Vigilante was originally designed as a carrier-borne nuclear bomber, but it was as a reconnaissance aircraft that it saw combat in Vietnam, where its only defense was its tremendous speed.

The RA-5C was first deployed to southeast Asia with RVAH-5 aboard the USS RANGER during August of 1964. During that time the Vigilante only flew missions over South Vietnam since the Navy was very reluctant to jeopardize the aircraft's sophisticated and very expensive equipment, should it go down over North Vietnam.

Eventually, the Vigilantes did go North and, in all, eighteen Vigilantes were lost in combat. Eleven to intense anti-aircraft fire when they were on post-strike photographic reconnaissance missions, two were shot down by SA-2 Guideline surface-to-air missiles (SAMs) and one was lost to an Atoll missile fired from a MiG-21 fighter. The other five were lost to unknown reasons, but all except one of these losses occurred over North Vietnam and were probably due to enemy action.

The Vigilantes and their crews provided invaluable information on enemy troop movements and concentrations gathered during route reconnaissance (Route Recces) missions over North Vietnam, one of the more common type of mission flown. In Vietnam the RA-5C Vigilante was an unqualified success. The Vigilantes were so valuable that, despite their high speed, they were usually accompanied by escorts of F-4 Phantoms on MIGCAP missions to keep the MiGs off of the RA-5Cs

The Vigilante always flew combat missions over land faster than Mach 1. Over North Vietnam, the RA-5C carried plenty of internal fuel and flew in maximum afterburner during every part of the mission. Most missions were flown over North Vietnam between 7,000 and 8,000 feet, at average speeds of Mach 1.1 to Mach 1.3 (it was not uncommon to hear escorting F-4 crews screaming at Vigilante pilots to slow down after the RA-5C had completed its mission, since the Phantoms, loaded down with missiles and fuel tanks, were rapidly being run out of fuel trying to keep up with the Vigilante).

For combat missions, the Vigilante was always the last aircraft to be launched on a cycle during flight operations since the RA-5C had the speed and fuel to easily catch up with the rest of the strike package. The Vigilante was never armed over North Vietnam, their main asset was speed, very high speed. The RA-5C would come in clean, very fast, approaching the target from any direction, and low (7,000 to 8, 000 feet). The North Vietnamese gunners did not have

A RA-5C of Heavy Seven (RVAH-7) comes aboard USS KITTYHAWK after a combat mission over North Vietnam during 1972. The tail hook on the RA-5C was V shaped with the rear of the canoe protruding into the V. (Nicholas J. Waters III)

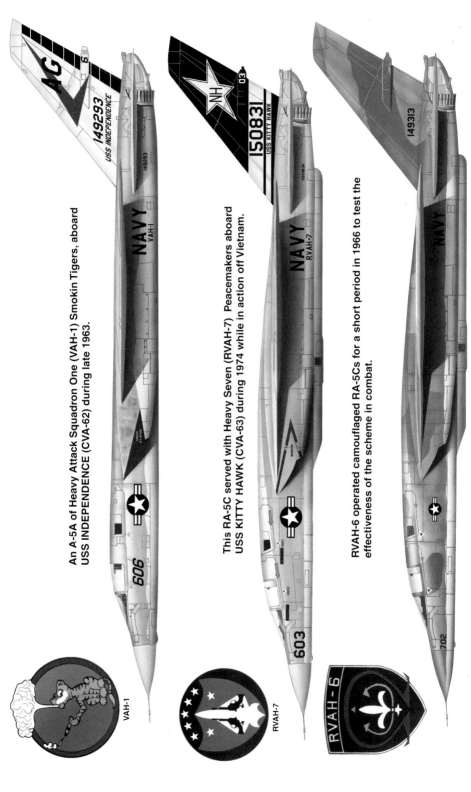

An A-5A of Heavy Attack Squadron One (VAH-1) Smokin Tigers, aboard USS INDEPENDENCE (CVA-62) during late 1963.

This RA-5C served with Heavy Seven (RVAH-7) Peacemakers aboard USS KITTY HAWK (CVA-63) during 1974 while in action off Vietnam.

RVAH-6 operated camouflaged RA-5Cs for a short period in 1966 to test the effectiveness of the scheme in combat.

VAH-1

RVAH-7

RVAH-6

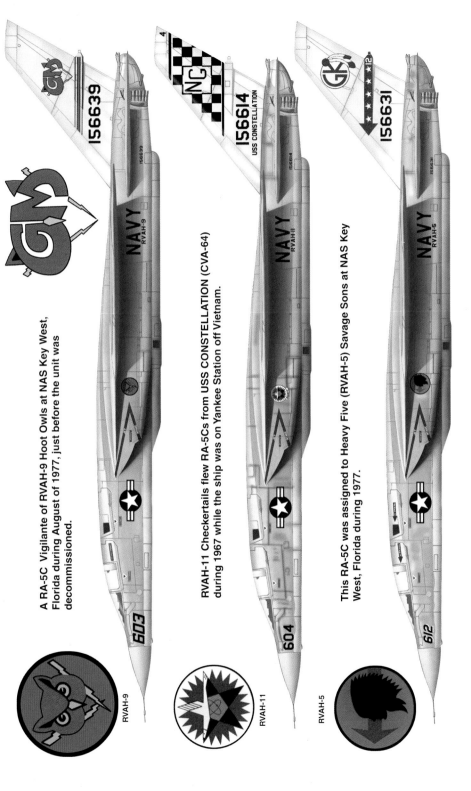

A RA-5C Vigilante of RVAH-9 Hoot Owls at NAS Key West, Florida during August of 1977, just before the unit was decommissioned.

RVAH-9

RVAH-11 Checkertails flew RA-5Cs from USS CONSTELLATION (CVA-64) during 1967 while the ship was on Yankee Station off Vietnam.

RVAH-11

This RA-5C was assigned to Heavy Five (RVAH-5) Savage Sons at NAS Key West, Florida during 1977.

RVAH-5

Photographers Mates position a camera module for loading into the forward camera bay of station four in the reconnaissance "canoe" of a RA-5C. Station four could carry a variety of cameras in the KA range from the 3 inch focal length KA-57 to the 18 inch focal length KA-58A panoramic camera. (Tailhook)

a lot of time to draw a bead on them (although one squadron commander had the unlucky distinction of being hit in the same spot on the aircraft (the radome), by the same type shell (57MM) while flying separate missions to Haiphong). Additionally, the RA-5C did not have to fly directly over the target to obtain Bomb Damage Assessment

This RA-5C of Heavy Nine (RVAH-9) caught the number two wire aboard USS RANGER (CVA-61) during combat operations in the South China Sea in December of 1968. From the smoke coming from the starboard main landing gear wheel, it is believed that the aircraft probably suffered a locked brake. This was the second Vietnam deployment for the Hoot Owls. (John Calhoun III)

A RA-5C (BuNo 156613) of RVAH-5 on the ramp of a NAS during August of 1973, between deployments aboard USS RANGER (CVA-61). The tail was White with Red lettering. The arrow insignia was Red with White stars. (Author)

(BDA) photographs due to the high quality of the oblique camera systems on board (on one mission the vertical shots taken of a target made it appear that the target had not been hit; however, the oblique shots of the same target revealed that every window in the building had been blown out. The bomb, a Walleye TV guided weapon, had been guided through a window, leaving the roof intact). The high speed and maneuverability of the Vigilante proved an outstanding value during combat in Vietnam with the ability to out-maneuver SAM missiles being frequently demonstrated. In one of its deployments to Vietnam, VAH-13 flew 125 missions over the Hanoi/Haiphong Harbor area with only

A RA-5C (BuNo 150835) of RVAH-5 was sling loaded aboard USS AMERICA (CVA-66) at Pier 12, Naval Operating Base, Norfolk, Virginia on 11 October 1965. Six days later, on 17 October, this Vigilante was lost at sea. (USN via Jim Goodall)

A BDA (Bomb Damage Assessment) reconnaissance photograph of Vinh airfield in North Vietnam on 4 May 1968. The Photographic Intelligenceman has annotated a line of bomb craters across the runway with White dashed lines. The code in the upper corner reveals that this was taken by a RA-5C of RVAH-6 aboard USS RANGER (CVA-61). The camera used was the forward oblique (KA-51 6 inch focal length) and the photo was frame five of the run. (John Calhoun III)

A RVAH-13 Vigilante banks away over the South China Sea revealing the underside of the RA-5C's reconnaissance canoe and V shaped tail hook. The canoe held many sensors, both optical and electronic. During 1974, the Bats were on a Western Pacific (WESTPAC) cruise aboard USS RANGER (CVA-61). (USN)

The basic reconnaissance canoe on the RA-5C was all the same; however, sensor station four could accommodate a wide variety of cameras and sensors. A close look at these two Vigilantes of RVAH-7 reveals different camera systems mounted in sensor station four. (USN via Nicholas J. Waters III)

A RA-5C of Heavy Five banks away from another RVAH-5 Vigilante over the Mediterranean. They were embarked in USS AMERICA (CVA-66) for its 1967 Med cruise. The aircraft in the background is equipped with an electronic flasher pod for night photography. In combat, the flasher pod was rarely used, because it gave away the aircraft's position to enemy gunners. Most night combat missions were flown with SLAR or infrared. (USN via Jim Goodall)

Electronic Flasher Pod

RA-5C

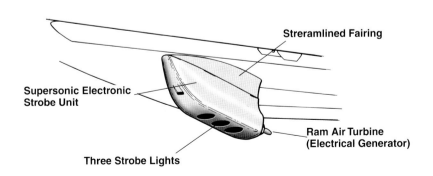

Streramlined Fairing

Supersonic Electronic
Strobe Unit

Ram Air Turbine
(Electrical Generator)

Three Strobe Lights

Everything down and dirty, a RA-5C of RVAH-11 Checkertails prepares to trap. Heavy Eleven was one of the squadrons that experimented with camouflage color schemes on their Vigilantes. The schemes differed from aircraft to aircraft with no standard being set before the project was abandoned. (Tailhook)

two incidences of damage from ground fire.

One of the early missions of the Vigilante squadrons was to completely map-survey North and South Vietnam. In response to a bombing mistake that was found to be directly attributed to inaccurate maps, the RA-5Cs generated optical imagery of the entire Vietnamese country, both North and South. This was accomplished without extraordinary difficulty and in less than two weeks, quickly building confidence in the aircraft and its systems.

Vigilantes over North Vietnam incurred the highest loss rate of any Naval aircraft in the war. Although the RA-5Cs primary mission of pre/post strike reconnaissance was simple in principle, they were extremely dangerous in practice. The basic mission was to obtain photography of targets, both before and after a strike mission. The pre-strike mission was usually uneventful, but it did not take long for the North Vietnamese to figure out that shortly after a strike mission, a Vigilante would be overhead on a post strike mission. Most RA-5C losses were during post strike missions.

There were thirty-one combat-zone deployments of the Vigilante squadrons to Vietnam. RVAH-5 and RVAH 6 each logged

five combat deployments, RVAH-1, 7, 11 and 13 each logged four deployments, RVAH-12 had three and RVAH-9 logged two. Only two Vigilante squadrons never deployed to Vietnam, RVAH-3, due to its capacity as the replacement air crew training unit and Heavy Fourteen, which had a permanent attachment to the Sixth Fleet in the Mediterranean.

During the early period of Vietnam operations, Vigilante squadrons deployed with six aircraft. As the war progressed, this figure began declining, first to five, then to four and finally, by 1974/75, to three aircraft per squadron. Additionally, it was not uncommon for one aircraft to be a "hangar queen", used to provide parts to keep the other two operational. With the aircraft out of production, spare parts were a major problem for the maintenance crews in the squadrons.

Editor's Note:

As a Photographic Intelligenceman First Class (PT1) and Multi-Sensor Interpretation (MSI) supervisor in the Integrated Operational Intelligence Center (IOIC) aboard USS KITTY HAWK (CVA-63) during the period 1970-1974, I had a personal relationship with the aircrews and

This RA-5C (BuNo 150834) of RVAH-13 carried a freshly applied camouflage scheme of Medium Green (FS34079), Tan (FS30219), and Olive Drab (FS34102) on the uppersurfaces with the undersurfaces remaining in Gloss White. (Tailhook)

support personnel of two RA-5C squadrons, RVAH-6 Fleurs and RVAH-7, Peacemakers during three combat deployments off Vietnam.

One of the primary systems during this period was the KA-58A low altitude panoramic camera. This outstanding camera system was capable of bringing back 2,500 feet of five inch film on a single mission, in addition there were also forward oblique and vertical cameras on board the Vigilante to record the mission route. Readout of this film for intelligence and targeting information was the responsibility of the MSI section of the IOIC. Normally one PT (we had only four qualified and experienced PTs assigned plus assistants) was assigned to each mission

A RA-5C of RVAH-13 caught an arresting wire aboard USS KITTYHAWK (CVA-63) during 1966. The camouflage was non standard and was only used for a short period of time. (Tailhook)

33

The linear bomb bay between the engines could also be used for specially designed air-to-air buddy refueling store which enabled any variant A-5 to act as a tanker. These Vigilantes of VAH-1 demonstrate refueling techniques while operating off USS INDEPENDENCE (CVA-62 during 1962). (Tailhook)

from planning to the final report. With so much film coming back, it was not uncommon for first phase readout of a target rich area to take twenty-four to thirty-six hours. The initial readout was done quickly from the film shot by the forward oblique camera to make a mission trace (route map of the mission) and to catch fleeting targets for possible strike. Afterward a more detailed readout was performed against a list of pre-existing targets, plus being always on the look-out for targets of opportunity. The longest mission I personally had was one that involved a route reconnaissance mission from Haiphong to just outside Hanoi. Due to the number of known targets that required status reporting (airfields, bridges, etc) this mission

took nearly forty-eight hours to complete.

One of the most rewarding missions that I recall was one planned and flown to locate and target North Vietnamese coastal defense guns that were firing on our destroyers operating on the gun line just off the North Vietnamese coast. We put one Vigilante over the area at high level to stir up the guns (they would move if they felt that they had been spotted), then followed it up with a second aircraft a short while later. The film from this second RA-5C caught the guns relocating and a strike was called in on them, destroying a number of the sites before they could move a second time.

During the 1972 cruise aboard KITTY HAWK, RVAH-7 was instrumental in pro-

Buddy Refueling Kit

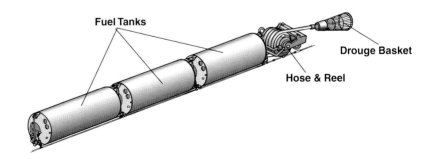

The plane captain assists the RAN as he climbs into the rear cockpit of a RA-5C of RVAH-6 aboard USS KITTYHAWK (CV-63) during 1976. This aircraft is equipped with the LEX which identifies it as one of the J79-GE-10 powered late production RA-5Cs. The tail in the foreground belongs to an A-7E of VA-195 Dambusters. (Larry Mullaly)

The flight crew of this RA-5C of Heavy Six (RVAH-6 Fleurs) await their turn for launch from USS KITTYHAWK (CVA-63) during February of 1968, with the canopies open. The aircraft in the background are F-4 Phantoms of VF-114 and VF-213. (Larry Mullaly)

A RA-5C of RVAH-6 Fleurs flying off USS RANGER (CVA-61) took this photograph of Vinh Airfield in southern North Vietnam on 4 May 1968. The extremely clear and crisp photography obtained by the RA-5C enabled photo interpreters to identify two occupied Anti-Aircraft Artillery (AAA) sites, both of which appear to have been attacked with Cluster Bomb Units (CBUs). The code sequence VT FR 16 identifies this as frame 16 from the vertical camera. (John Calhoun III)

viding intelligence on enemy movements during the North Vietnamese Easter invasion of South Vietnam. Photography gathered in low level missions over Hoa caught NVA tanks (PT-76s) swimming the river near the town, again enabling strike aircraft to find and hit these mobile targets before they were able to disperse into the countryside. Even though we had numerous problems with the PECM (Passive Electronic Countermeasures) and infrared systems on the RA-5C (due to their complex nature and difficulty in performing proper maintenance aboard ship) the optical camera systems always came through. When the RA-5C was retired, it left a huge gap in the tactical reconnaissance capability of the carrier force, one that took a long time to fill.

A RA-5C (BuNo 150831) of RVAH-7 Peacemakers takes on fuel from a KA-6D Intruder tanker from VA-52 during early 1974. This was Heavy Seven's last cruise aboard USS KITTYHAWK (CV-63). During this cruise the ship operated off Vietnam and made a trip into the Indian Ocean. (Nicholas J. Waters III)

Deck crewmen on the USS AMERICA (CVA-66) hook up a Vigilante of RVAH-5 to the bow catapult in preparation for launch on a photo recon flight on 15 October 1965. The supersonic flasher pod under the port wing was developed specifically for the RA-5C for use in night photo missions. (USN via Jim Goodall)

Carrying AE tailcodes (identifying them as being assigned to an East Coast Air Group) two RA-5Cs of RVAH-5 fly a loose formation over the Mediterranean Sea during 1967. The squadron was based aboard USS AMERICA (CVA- 66). (USN via Jim Goodall)

A RA-5C (BuNo 146696) (the fifth Vigilante built) of RVAH-1, catches the number one arresting wire aboard USS SARATOGA (CVA-60) on 11 May 1969. The Vigilante was one of the heaviest aircraft ever to operate off of an aircraft carrier deck. (USN)

(Above) RVAH-3 was the Replacement Air Group (RAG) for the Vigilante community, responsible for training crews to go into active units. This A-5C (BuNo 156640) was conducting a training flight over the Florida countryside. The aircraft was lost on just such a mission on 3 October 1967. (John Calhoun III)

The underslung reconnaissance canoe is clearly visible on this RA-5C (BuNo 156624) of RVAH-5. The Savage Sons were attached to the USS CONSTELLATION (CVA-64), which was homeported at NAS North Island, San Diego, California on 3 August 1974 . (USN)

A RA-5C of RVAH-7 Peacemakers just after being catapulted off of the waist catapult of USS KITTYHAWK (CVA-63) operating in the South China Sea during 1974. A combination of large flaps, leading edge slats, and powerful engines allowed the heavy Vigilante to operate off of aircraft carriers. (Nicholas J. Waters III)

With its outer wing panels folded, a RA-5C of Heavy Seven (RVAH-7) shares the deck edge with a F-4J Phantom II of VF-114 aboard USS KITTYHAWK off the coast of Vietnam during 1972. The Phantom was armed with AIM-9 Sidewinder missiles on the inboard pylons. Both aircraft are tied down with tow bars in place. (Nicholas J. Waters III)

A RA-5C of RVAH-11 takes on fuel from a EKA-3B Skywarrior of VAQ-131 high over the Pacific. Both aircraft were operating from USS KITTYHAWK (CVA-63) during a combat cruise off Vietnam in early 1969. For RVAH-11, it would be their third combat cruise. (John Calhoun III)

39

Commander C.C. Smith, Jr., and Lieutenant John E. Calhoun III, climb aboard their Vigilante for their famous "Hanoi Hilton" mission over the North Vietnamese capitol city. The film obtained from this mission allowed photographic interpreters to positively locate the infamous POW camp in downtown Hanoi. At the time, the squadron was flying off of the USS RANGER (CVA-61). (John Calhoun III)

Post Vietnam

The North American Columbus division engineering team proposed several variants of the A-5 to the USAF's Aerospace Defense Command as a replacement for the Convair F-106A interceptor. One proposal was developed under the name Retaliator and was powered by two J79-GE-10 turbojet engines and a Rocketdyne XLR46-NA-2 liquid-fuel rocket to boost high altitude performance. The Air Force initially showed some interest in the Retaliator but, in the event, the project was dropped.

Around 1972, North American proposed placing a third J79-GE-10 engine in the weapons bay, for an advanced variant of the Vigilante optimized to meet an Air Force interceptor requirements. It was estimated to be capable of speeds in excess of Mach 2.5 and altitudes of over 80,000 feet. The aircraft was envisioned to be armed with as many as six AIM-54 Phoenix AAMs (the

A RA-5C (BuNo 156620) of RVAH-1 being pre-flighted by ground crews during August of 1973. The Smokin' Tigers had just returned from a Mediterranean cruise aboard USS AMERICA (CVA-66). (Ron McNeil)

RVAH-1 Smokin' Tigers operated this Vigilante off of the USS JOHN F. KENNEDY (CVA-67). It was common for Vigilantes to change their tail codes due to the fact that the squadrons shifted from air group to air group to fill the reconnaissance needs of the fleet. The RA-5C units had some of the more colorful markings in the U.S. Navy at the time. (Hugh Muir)

The USS Enterprise (CVAN-65) was the home for RVAH-1 Smokin' Tigers, during the later half of 1976 and for this deployment they carried an NK tail code. The ventral reconnaissance canoe was over half the total length of the Vigilante. (via Hugh Muir)

This RA-5C of RVAH-3, the Replacement Air Group (RAG) for the Vigilante community carries the unit's Red and White tail markings. These were the final style of markings carried on Heavy Three just before the unit was decommissioned on 17 August 1979. (Author)

same missile that arms the F-14 carried semi-internal on the fuselage undersurface. Again this project was not taken up by the Air Force.

As the number of RA-5Cs in active squadrons continued to shrink and the problem of spare parts continued to grow, the Navy began to disestablish squadrons, pass-

A RA-5C (BuNo 156621) of RVAH-5 during the squadron's last Vietnam cruise in 1973. Heavy Five was assigned to the USS RANGER (CVA-61) at the time. This Vigilante has a very weathered appearance where maintenance personnel have touched up the Gloss Gull Gray paint on the fuselage sides. (Hugh Muir)

A RA-5C (BuNo 156631) of RVAH-5 Savage Sons on the ramp at Naval Air Station Key West during 1977. The unit insignia was visible just behind the air intake. It had a Blue background outlined in Black with a Black Indian-head profile over a Red arrow. The fin was White with Black numbers, a Red arrow with White stars and a Red tail code. (Jim Mesko)

A RA-5C Vigilante (BuNo 156608) of Heavy Five (RVAH-5) Savage Sons shares the ramp at Atlanta, Georgia with Army OV-1 Mohawks during 1977. The unit insignia is carried on the fuselage side just under the Leading Edge Extension (LEX). (via Hugh Muir)

A RA-5C (BuNo 156624) of RVAH-6 on the ramp with the station four camera pod missing from the reconnaissance canoe. This Vigilante is now on display at the Naval Aviation Museum in Pensacola, Florida. (Hugh Muir)

ing their aircraft on to those still in service. The first to be decommissioned was Heavy Fourteen (RVAH-14) Eagle Eyes which ceased operations on 1 May 1974. The unit had been in service for six years, having been established on 1 February 1968 at NAS Sanford.

The next unit to go was RVAH-11 Checkertails. This unit had a number of firsts to its credit, it was the first RA-5C unit to photograph Haiphong Harbor once operations resumed after the 1968 bombing halt. The unit disestablished on 1 June 1975.

One year later, RVAH-13 Bats, which had received its first RA-5C on 5 October 1964, were disestablished (30 June 1976). They

RVAH-6 Fleurs flew this RA-5C (BuNo. 156638) while assigned to the USS KITTYHAWK (CVA-63). This is one of the late-production Vigilantes equipped with J79-GE-10 engines. (Author)

RVAH-7 Peacemakers of the Fleet operated this RA-5C during the Summer of 1975. The 601 side number identifies the aircraft as being assigned to the squadron commander. The unit was based on USS FORRESTAL (CVA-59) at that time. (Hugh Muir)

ceased flying shortly after returning from their last Med cruise aboard USS INDEPENDENCE (CVA-62).

Two units were closed down on 30 September 1977, RVAH-5 Savage Sons and RVAH-9 Hoot Owls. In 1978, RVAH 6 Fluers (20 October) joined the list of decommissioned units.

1979 was the last year for Vigilante operations, and the remaining squadrons were all decommissioned during this year. RVAH 1 Smokin' Tigers was first leaving the fleet on 19 January, it was followed by RVAH-12 Speartips (2 July), RVAH-3 Sea Dragons (17 August) and finally RVAH-7 Peacemakers (28 September 1979. The last Navy RA-5C flight took place on 20 November 1979), when Lieutenant Westmoreland and Lieutenant Commander Plunkett flew BuNo

156608 from Naval Air Station Key West Florida, to Davis Monthan Air Force Base. The last official act was the disestablishment of the Wing (Attack Wing One), which took place on 7 January 1980 at NAS Key West.

A total of thirty-six RA-5Cs found their way to Davis Monthan AFB where they were placed in storage. Of these, eight were later transferred to the New Mexico Institute of Mining and Technology storage area at Socorro, New Mexico, for use as targets. Five were transferred to the Naval Weapons Center at China Lake, California again for use as targets. One such RA-5C target was destroyed during testing of the Tomahawk cruise missile.

This was the last color and markings scheme used by RVAH-7 Peacemakers of the Fleet, during September of 1979. A short time later, the squadron was decommissioned, at the time RVAH-7 was the last Vigilante squadron still flying. (Hugh Muir)

45

This Hoot Owls (RVAH-9) Vigilante was modified with the J79-GE-10 engines. The key identification feature is the Leading Edge Extension (LEX) that runs to the edge of the air intake and the shape of the intake itself. (Hugh Muir)

A RA-5C (BuNo 156615) of RVAH-9 Hoot Owls was the only Vigilante squadron to make a cruise aboard the nuclear aircraft carrier USS NIMITZ (CVN-68). The squadron deployed aboard NIMITZ during late 1976 for a cruise with the 6th Fleet in the Mediterranean. The F-4J Phantom II in the background belongs to VMFA-333, a Marine Corps fighter squadron. (Hugh Muir)

AA was the tail code of Heavy Twelve during its Mediterranean cruise in early 1969 aboard USS FORRESTAL (CVA-59). BuNo 150829 takes on fuel from a VAH-10 KA-3B Skywarrior high above the sea. (USN via Charles B. Meyer)

This RA-5C (BuNo 156640) of RVAH-12 had just returned from a Vietnam cruise in May of 1975. The squadron had been deployed aboard USS ENTERPRISE (CVN-65). The nose cone has a special marking consisting of a Red flash with six White stars. (Hugh Muir)

In February of 1969 RVAH-12 had just returned from a Mediterranean cruise aboard the USS SARATOGA (CVA-60). The RA-5C (BuNo 156640) carried the Roman numeral XII on the fin in Red. This was a repeat of the squadron number (RVAH-12). (Author)

47

A RA-5C (BuNo 156624) undergoes maintenance in a hangar at NAS Key West in May of 1977. RVAH-12 was assigned to USS INDEPENDENCE (CVA-62) and was preparing to deploy on a Mediterranean cruise with the 6th Fleet. (Larry Mullaly)

This RA-5C (BuNo 156638) of RVAH-12 carried BiCentennial markings during early 1976. This was the squadron commanders aircraft which carried a Red radome with a White flash with six Blue stars. BuNo 156638 was also one of the last Vigilantes built. (Hugh Muir)

These were the markings carried by RA-5Cs of RVAH-11 Checkertails during their last deployment aboard USS SARATOGA (CVA-60). The ship deployed to the Sixth Fleet in the Mediterranean during early 1975 and upon return the unit was decommissioned. BuNo. 156642 was the next to the last Vigilante built. (Hugh Muir)

A RA-5C (BuNo 156639) of RVAH-12 on the ramp at Naval Air Station Key West, Florida on 14 April 1979. The Speartips of RVAH-12 were based aboard USS SARATOGA (CVA-60) for their last cruise. After they returned to Key West the unit was disestablished on 2 July 1979. The rail markings were (top to bottom) Red, White, Blue with a Red XII and Black tail code and BuNo. (Doug Remington)

The Bat insignia of RVAH-13 was clear and proudly displayed on the fuselage side just behind the air intake. The background was Orange as was the stripe on the White tail and the bat was Black. (Author)

Early in 1976, the Bats of RVAH-13 were aboard the USS INDEPENDENCE (CVA-62) for their last cruise. The squadron was disestablished in June of 1976. (Hugh Muir)

This RA-5C (BuNo 148925) carries the Eagle Eyes squadron insignia of RVAH -14 on the nose with the reproduction of the squadron patch being carried on the fuselage side just behind the air intake. The background was Light Blue, the eagle and talons were Black and the rays coming from the eyes were Red. (Hugh Muir)